FIGURE SKATING

MARGARET RYAN

FIGURE SKATING

FRANKLIN WATTS 1987

NEW YORK   LONDON   TORONTO   SYDNEY

A FIRST BOOK

Illustrations by Holly Stuart Hughes

Photographs courtesy of: AP/Wide World Photos: cover, pp. 58, 64 (top); World
Figure Skating Hall of Fame and Museum Collection: pp. 11, 12; UPI/
Bettmann Newsphotos: pp. 15, 57, 64 (bottom), 66; Photo Researchers, Inc.:
p. 27 (Yan Lukas); International Management Group: p. 65 (David Leonardi).

Library of Congress Cataloging-in-Publication Data

Ryan, Margaret.
Figure skating.

(A First book)
Summary: An introduction to figure skating,
including descriptions of equipment, instructions
in beginning steps and more advanced tricks, tips
on developing style, information on competitions,
and a history of the sport.
1. Skating—Juvenile literature.   [1. Ice skating]
I. Title.
GV850.4.R93 1987   796.91   87-10532
ISBN 0-531-10383-8

CONTENTS

To the memories of
Walter Molnar and Eugene Helvig,
two fine skating gentlemen,
and to my mom, Anne J. Ryan,
for driving me to lessons.

1
INTRODUCTION TO THE ICE

You turn on the television and hear fiery gypsy music. You watch a woman in a short, sequined dress flash across an expanse of ice. She leaps, turns, lands. She is as graceful and beautiful as any ballerina, and somehow more powerful. The crowd roars applause.

Or you turn on the television and hear the beat of rock music. A man in a black jumpsuit, with a brilliant sapphire shirt underneath, dances past. The announcer says the skater has just done a flawless triple Salchow. To you, it looks like he invented flight. Once again, the crowd goes wild.

Or maybe you've been to an ice show. You've seen couples dancing together on ice, along with clowns, cartoon characters, soloists, and chorus lines, in a spectacle whose energy gives you shivers and drives you, applauding, to your feet.

Perhaps you're one of the lucky ones who has been given ice skates for a birthday or holiday. You head out for the local frozen pond or the nearest rink. In the center of the ice, dressed in nothing more flashy than a sweatsuit or a sweater and a pair of jeans, you see someone about your own age perform a perfect sit spin, a Russian split, and several flawless jumps.

9

Whether you're drawn to figure skating by glamour, showmanship, athletics, your competitive nature ("I could do that"), or a "What the heck, let's give this a try" attitude, you're soon hooked. And you want to know more.

WHAT'S IN A NAME?

Your first question might well be, "Why is it called figure skating?" When skating was developing in Holland, Dutch skaters discovered that their blades left marks, or tracings, on the ice. They began drawing pictures, or "figures," as they skated and even staged competitions in which they would trace flowers, stars, and faces on the ice. The most precise and prettiest ice drawing would win.

Today, skaters who compete are required to trace figures on the ice, too. These exercises leave tracings that look more like arithmetic lessons than art, as skaters trace variations of the figure eight. This part of the competition, called the compulsory, or school, figures, is not often shown on television. While figures demonstrate a skater's precision, discipline, and skill, they're not nearly as colorful as the freestyle skating that makes it to your screen.

The term "freestyle" is somewhat misleading. In most skating competitions, a skater must perform two freestyle programs. One, called the short program, is also known as the compulsory free program—a contradiction in terms. The short program must include specific jumps, spins, and other moves, and these cannot be changed. During the other freestyle, or long, program, a skater is free to change a move if necessary during rehearsal or competition. But every move has usually been planned and practiced again and again.

Skating in Holland in the 1870s

*Jackson Haines,
the father of the
International Style
of skating*

SKATING IN AMERICA

Skating has been a favorite winter pastime in North America for well over a hundred years. In fact, an American named Jackson Haines is called the father of the International Style of skating. This style is the forerunner of the skating we watch today, with dancelike movements done to music. Haines, who became famous during the 1860s, was the first to skate to music and the first to use the movements of ballet on ice.

Since Jackson Haines, many skaters have contributed to the growth of the American skating style. Sonja Henie, Tenley Albright, Carol Heiss, Janet Lynn, Peggy Fleming, Dorothy Hamill, and Debi Thomas are just a few of the women whose champion skating has shaped the art and sport of freestyle skating.

Men whose skating has pushed the boundaries of art and sport include Dick Button, Hayes Jenkins, David Jenkins, Don Jackson, Scott Hamilton, Toller Cranston, John Curry, and Robin Cousins.

PAIRS AND ICE DANCING

In addition to the great solo skaters, many pair-skating and ice-dancing couples have added to the growth of figure skating. In pair skating, a man and a woman skate together, performing many of the same freestyle skating moves single skaters do. In addition, there are special pair moves: pair lifts, spins, throws, and the haunting death spiral. To perform the death spiral, the man swings his partner while he remains still. The woman is almost horizontal to the ice as she revolves around her partner. Often the woman's hair will brush the ice as she moves at great speed on the very edge of her blade.

Lyudmila and Oleg Protopopov are perhaps the most famous modern pair-skating team. These two Russian skaters won the pair-skating event in both the 1964 and the 1968 Winter

Olympic games. Their elegant, classical lines brought true sophistication to pair skating.

Ice dancing is different from pair skating. Ice dancing does not feature lifts, spins, and death spirals, but sequences of intricate footwork and elaborate partnering positions that complement the music and express its rhythm and mood. Standardized ice dances include the Dutch waltz, the foxtrot, the blues, the tango, and the American waltz.

The British have been very successful in ice-dancing competition. Recently, British ice dancers Jayne Torvill and Christopher Dean, Gold Medal winners in 1982, 1983, and 1984, have popularized ice dancing as they toured the United States.

GETTING STARTED

As you begin skating, keep in mind that every champion began by learning the basics. This book will help you to understand, and perhaps master, some of those beginning moves. But figure skating is a rich and interesting sport, and a book can help only so much. Reading about skating won't be enough. There are several ways you can learn more.

Skate—There's no teacher like experience. Every half hour you spend on the ice, every time you fall and get back up again, will be a lesson in itself.

Watch—Keep your eye on skaters at your rink or pond. Go to ice shows. Watch competitions on television. You will see how a good skater holds her hands, or how a champion bends his knees. Remember those positions when you return to the ice and practice them for yourself.

Ask—People who skate well are often generous with hints, tips, maybe even lessons. It's flattering to be asked, "How do you do that?" or "Could you show me how?" Granted, not everyone is open, friendly, and willing to share, but many skaters are. You might as well ask.

Lyudmila and Oleg Protopopov, the Olympic pairs figure skating champions at the 1964 and 1968 Winter Olympics

Take lessons—Private lessons tend to be expensive but well worth it as you become more advanced. For beginners, group lessons from a professional can be surprisingly affordable, effective, and fun. If no group lessons are available in your area, maybe you can put together a small number of friends and hire a pro for an hour or two until you get the hang of things.

Finally, don't forget to have fun!

2
EQUIPMENT

Modern figure skates are available in several types. Some are designed for school figures, others for ice dancing, and others are for all-purpose skating. But all are made from the same basic parts: boots and steel blades.

Professional skaters, and many serious amateurs, buy boots and blades separately. If your feet have stopped growing, or if you're involved in serious competition, you might buy them separately, too.

But most people who begin skating buy boots and blades already assembled. Here are some things to look for when buying skates.

BOOTS

First, what material are the boots made from? Leather is the material of choice. It is flexible even when cold. Air can pass through leather, which allows perspiration to evaporate and keeps your feet dry. Leather boots tend to fit better than boots made of other materials. Some leather boots are lined and generously padded with foam. Others are simply unlined leather.

Vinyl boots lined with leather, and boots made of all vinyl, are another option. Vinyl boots are less expensive than leather—a consideration if you are growing rapidly and your skates need to be replaced often. Many people, however, feel that vinyl is too stiff to make a comfortable boot. Again, try them. You will probably prefer leather-lined vinyl boots to the all-vinyl variety. But even all-vinyl boots could be right for you now. When your feet stop growing, though, you will want to invest in all-leather boots.

Fit is your next consideration. Snug-fitting boots will give you the support you need to skate. Expect to buy skates a half to a full size smaller than your regular shoe size if you are a girl. Boys' skates seem to run truer to shoe size, but you may still wear boots a half size smaller than your shoes. You'll know the skates are your size if your toes come close to the end of the boot.

When you try skates on, wear one pair of thin socks or tights. Thick socks will keep you from getting the snug fit you need. They won't keep your feet warm; they'll just make your feet fat. If you wear thick socks, you will have to lace your boots very tightly to get good support. You run the risk of cutting off circulation, which will make your feet colder and give you pins-and-needles numbness.

Good boots should offer good support, both for your foot and for your ankle. New boots should feel a little stiff when you try them on, and they should keep your ankles straight up, not wobbly, when laced. Some skaters improve almost overnight when they switch from floppy-ankled rental skates to supportive boots. If your ankles collapse while you're trying to skate, give new boots a try.

To check the fit of boots, stand in them and try to move your heel up and down. You shouldn't be able to: the heel should feel snug. Your toes need a little room to wiggle, but not too much. Skates should fit like gloves, not like galoshes.

18

BLADES

The front of a figure skating blade is ridged, or toothed. This is called the toe pick. It is used in many freestyle skating moves, such as jumps and a very few spins.

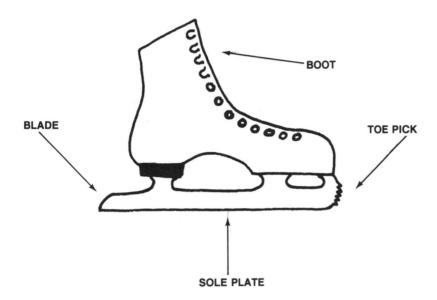

The rest of the blade looks curved when seen from the side. Actually, the blade is part of a circle with a diameter of about six feet. This curve makes possible many of the graceful moves and turns we admire when we watch professional skaters.

If you look at a cross-section of a blade, you will see that it, too, is part of a circle—a much smaller circle, though. This circle is called the hollow. The blade is ground, or sharpened, in this way so that you have two edges to skate on each blade. These are called the inside and the outside edges and will be discussed in more detail later.

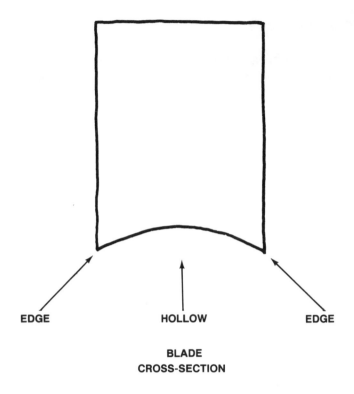

EDGE **HOLLOW** **EDGE**

BLADE
CROSS-SECTION

Figure skating blades should be made of good-quality steel. Many are chromium plated, so they look shiny. Sometimes steel blades are marked: they might say "tempered steel" or "Sheffield steel." You will have to pay a little more for skates with steel blades, but it will be worth it.

Many children's skates now available have blades made of lighter metals, perhaps a combination of aluminum, nickel, or zinc. These blades have a dull finish and dull edges. They cannot be properly sharpened and they tend to slip rather than bite into the ice.

Don't waste money on double runners. They won't teach you anything about gliding or balance.

RENT OR BUY?

Rental skates are available at most rinks. It's a good idea to rent skates the first few times, until you decide whether skating is for you. Once you've decided to stick with skating, though, you really should get your own skates. Rental skates are usually built to last, not to provide comfort, fit, or support. You will learn more—and more quickly—if you have your own skates.

SHARPENING

In order to keep the edges on your blades, you will have to have your skates sharpened from time to time. How often you have your skates sharpened depends on how much you skate—and how well you treat your blades. For many amateur skaters, once a year is enough. If you skate frequently, though, you may need to have your skates sharpened as often as once a month.

When you do have your skates sharpened, please go to a rink, a pro shop, or a skate store to have it done. Blades can be ruined if they're sharpened improperly, and it's hard to skate if your edges aren't just right.

OTHER EQUIPMENT

Skates are the only equipment you *must* have in order to start figure skating. But you will enjoy having a few other items that can help protect and extend the life of your skates.

Skate guards are covers for your blades. These are usually made of plastic, rubber, or wood. They protect your blades while you are off the ice and are a must if you must walk across wooden planks, stone, brick, or dirt—anything other than rubber matting—to get to the ice. Make sure you take them off before getting on the ice, though, or you will fall.

21

A skate bag is also a good idea. You can use a heavy plastic sack, a canvas tote bag, or the sort of bag airlines used to give away—whatever you feel comfortable with, whatever your skates fit into.

Put a piece of an old *towel* into your tote bag. You'll want to wipe your blades completely dry as soon as you leave the ice. This will prevent rust and protect your edges. You can then cover your blades with *terry cloth blade covers*, if you like.

OUTFITS

What you wear to skate in will be determined by where you skate and who you are.

Indoors. Girls usually wear the classic skating costume: a sweater, or a blouse, and jacket; a short skirt, flared or pleated from the hips; skin-colored tights (the heavier Orlon type are popular now); and trunks, which are similar to the bottom of a leotard, usually in the same color as your skirt. If you wear a leotard under your skirt and sweater, the bottom of the leotard can take the place of trunks. Leg warmers look nice over tights and can help keep you warm. Of course, if you'd rather, you can always wear pants. Stirrup pants work well for some people. Pants made of stretch materials are especially good, as are sweatpants.

Whatever you wear, try to select clothing that is lightweight, warm, and flexible.

Girls can wear a hat and gloves if they wish. No trailing scarves, please. And jewelry can be a hazard, especially if it is loose or falls off.

Although custom says men shouldn't wear hats at an indoor rink, hats are still a good idea for boys. They help to retain body heat and provide some protection for the head in case of falls. Sweatpants make good, comfortable bottoms. Jeans are also fine—just be sure they're loose enough so you can move.

Above the waist, wear a shirt and sweater or jacket. Turtlenecks are warm and very comfortable. By all means, wear gloves if you wish. Again, skip trailing scarves. And you might want to remove any sharp items, such as keys, from your back pocket . . . you don't want to crash land on them.

Outdoors. When you're skating outdoors, your goal is warmth, not glamour. All the rink rules apply, but everything's subject to the weather. Hats are especially important outdoors. Most body heat is lost from the neck up, so a hat can really help keep you cozy. Gloves are usually needed. Some people find mittens warmer than gloves. If you're one of them, look for mittens designed for skiers; they will help keep your hands warm and dry.

Dress in thin layers. Layers trap heat and have the advantage of letting you adjust your clothing to both the temperature of the air and of your own body. Girls can wear several layers of tights to keep their legs warm. Some boys wear sweatpants over jeans for outdoors skating.

It's usually better to use a heavy sweater rather than a coat as your final outer layer. Even short jackets, when closed, can interfere with movement. And an open jacket can act like a sail, making it difficult to skate against the wind.

To keep your feet warm, you can wear insulated boot covers that slip on over your skates. These are available at many skating shops, sporting goods stores, and pro shops.

HOW TO LACE A SKATE

Now that you've got your outfit on, you're ready to lace up your skates. Lace tightly over your instep and tightest at the level of the ankle. Keep laces firm as you work your way up the hooks. At the top of the skate, the lacing should be fairly loose: if you can fit two fingers between your leg and the top of the boot, you've done it correctly. You want the lacing firm enough to hold you up, but not so tight that you cut off circulation.

When you reach the last hook, tie a solid bow. Then tuck the ends of your laces in, either under the lacings or between the boot and the tongue.

You may need to adjust the lacing a few times during every skating session. Don't be afraid to tighten or loosen your lacings as you warm up.

SKATE MAINTENANCE

Skates will last longer if they're properly cared for. Here are a few hints.

Keep your boots clean. Black marks can be taken off white boots with a little alcohol. Polish black boots and white boots the same way you polish shoes. Boot creams can be used on all colors to keep the leather supple.

You can also buy waterproof black polish for the soles of your skates. This is important if the soles of your boots are made of leather. It will keep the soles from getting soft and the blades from loosening. Vinyl soles need just an occasional cleaning with a damp cloth.

To protect your blades, always wear guards when you're off the ice, unless you're walking on rubber padding. Never wear guards on the ice—you'll fall. If you forget—and even professionals do it now and then—be sure to remove the guards before trying to stand up again and exit the ice.

As soon as you leave the ice, wipe your skates dry with the towel in your skate bag. If you don't, your blades will rust and dull. Don't store blades in the guards, which tend to hold moisture. You can cover the blades with terry-cloth blade covers, if you have them.

When you get home, take your skates out of your tote bag so they can dry. If the insides of your skates are damp from perspiration, unlace the skates, pull the tongues forward, and let them dry at room temperature in a well-ventilated area. Don't put skates too close to radiators or other heat sources, which will make the leather brittle.

Now that you have all your equipment in order, it's time to find some ice.

3
FINDING SOME ICE

There's no need to wait for winter, or to move up North, if you want to skate. Ice-skating rinks providing smooth artificial ice have been built across the United States and throughout Canada. Many operate 12 months a year. Of course, if you live in a northern climate, there's also real outside ice: a local pond, an artificial or natural lake, even a canal or river.

Each kind of ice has its own appeal. Artificial ice—whether indoor or outdoor—is safer. You don't have to worry about falling through. It's also smoother. The surface will be cleaned and maintained regularly.

Even so, skating on a frozen pond in winter, with a view of ice-silvered trees and clear blue sky overhead, the call of an occasional bird, or the sound of the wind, has its own charms. There's the thrill of black ice, the crack of hockey sticks, the fire

Skating in Central Park,
in New York City

by the bank, where your friends and neighbors roast marshmallows and sip hot cocoa.

There are drawbacks, of course. Maintaining a smooth skating surface is usually up to you. That means going to work with snow shovels before you get to the pleasure of skating. It can be a daunting task. And there's the definite question of safety.

SAFETY

Skating outdoors can be very dangerous, even life-threatening. You must never skate on outdoor ice unless

- YOU KNOW THE ICE IS SAFE,
- YOU ARE WITH A BUDDY, *AND*
- THERE IS ADULT SUPERVISION.

How do you know if the ice is safe? The season's first ice usually looks smooth. And it usually is—but it can also be thin and too weak to support the weight of even one skater. Black ice is usually solid, white ice less so, but there are no hard-and-fast rules. Rely on competent adults to tell you if the ice is safe; don't test for yourself.

Here are some other guidelines to help make outdoor skating safer.

Never skate outdoors alone. Even if the ice seems solid as a rock, a sudden thaw, a few hours of sunlight, or other factors could make it dangerous. It is important to have a companion while you skate outdoors. The buddy system could save your life: if you fall through, your friend can help you out or go for help. If you are skating alone and fall through, you might be trapped underwater, or go into shock.

Even with a buddy, skate close to shore.
Never skate at night.
Skate only on lakes or ponds where
there is adult supervision.

It's safest to skate where the water is less than waist-deep. Even if you do fall through, you can't go very far under.

If you see others skating on ice you know is not safe, warn them. Listen to others if they tell *you* the ice is dangerous.

If you fall through the ice, slide your arms across the ice at the edge of the break and kick hard, pushing your body forward, flat onto the ice. Climbing out by trying to raise yourself on the ice may break ice off the edges of the hole and get you nowhere. Once you are out of the water, don't try to stand. The ice may not hold your weight. Instead, roll to the shore and safety.

What if a friend falls in? Find something you can extend to him or her—a ladder, a pole, a branch, even a sturdy article of clothing such as a scarf or jacket. Approach the break in the ice carefully: lie flat on your belly and inch only close enough to reach the object you're holding to your friend. When your friend has grasped the object firmly, pull the skater to safety by inching backward carefully across the ice. If others are around, form a human chain by lying on the ice, one behind the other. Each person should grasp the ankles of the one in front.

Never stand while trying to rescue someone. Stay on your belly, so that your weight is evenly distributed over a large area. Once your friend is out of the water, have him or her roll across the ice to the safety of the shore.

What if a friend goes under and doesn't emerge? Mark the spot with an article of clothing and go *quickly* for help. Immediately give mouth-to-mouth resuscitation if the person is not breathing. Call for help.

After rescue, it's important to get the victim dry and warm as soon as possible. Seek medical attention.

The best cure, of course, is prevention. To repeat the basics:

- *DON'T SKATE OUTDOORS ALONE.*
- *DON'T SKATE WITHOUT ADULT SUPERVISION.*
- *DON'T SKATE AT NIGHT.*
- *DON'T SKATE ON ICE YOU'RE UNSURE OF.*

4 GETTING STARTED

As with most sports, it's a good idea to warm up and loosen up your muscles before you begin to skate. Being warmed up will make it easier for you to move correctly and will help prevent injuries.

Some skaters like to warm up by flexing every joint. Working through a routine that takes about fifteen minutes, they might begin with head rolls to limber neck muscles, do arm circles, then bend at the waist to both sides. To loosen the spine, some skaters roll down to touch the floor and up again slowly, while keeping the knees soft and slightly bent to prevent back injuries.

Many good workout programs are available on videocassette, audiotape, and in books. If you'd like to learn more about exercises that will help strengthen your muscles and keep you flexible, check into the variety of exercise information available.

FINDING YOUR BALANCE

Once you have your skates on, begin by just standing on the ice. At a rink, you might hold onto the rail, or "boards," as they're called at ice rinks.

When you're ready, let go. Simply stand still on the ice. Bend your knees slightly, being careful not to bend forward at the waist. It's important to keep your back upright and to keep your center of gravity—what you feel is the heaviest part of you—over both your feet. Also keep your shoulders slightly forward to keep you from falling backward.

Now try moving forward. You will probably walk at first: it's how you're used to moving, and it's okay. Just take tiny steps, being sure to pick up one foot and place it in front of the other. Take your steps slowly and carefully, and hold onto the rail as you go if you like. Concentrate on staying balanced, and keeping your weight over your feet.

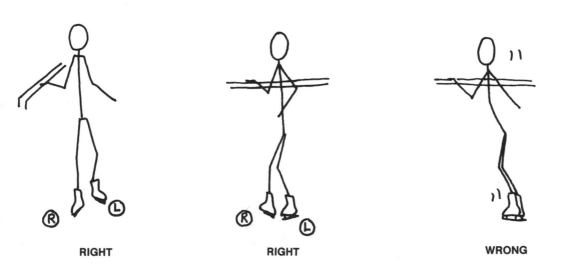

RIGHT   RIGHT   WRONG

Try not to lean forward from the waist; rather, keep your head over your hips, and bend from the knees, not from your middle. Putting your head too far forward—or back—will unbalance you.

Resist the temptation to hold onto a friend. Unless he or she is absolutely solid on skates, the two of you will be in more danger of falling together than you will be if you are skating alone.

Keep moving around the edge of the rink, close to the boards, in the direction of traffic.

If you are skating outdoors, try to find a small patch near the shore where you can move forward without getting in the way of the hockey game, the speedskaters, and the future Ice Capades hopeful practicing her triple Lutz.

If you feel self-conscious, remember that no one is born knowing how to figure-skate—it's all learned. And everyone else is busy keeping his or her balance. Skaters are used to seeing beginners around and won't be focusing on your attempts. Relax.

ABOUT FALLS

Everyone who learns to skate needs to learn how to fall. Everyone falls. Those who learn the most probably fall the most. Decide that it will happen, and learn how to do it right.

Falling on ice is both less and more painful than falling on a floor or the pavement. It's less painful because as you slide, some of the weight of the fall is absorbed. It's more, because you're going to get wet and cold where you and the ice make contact.

The best advice about falling is often hard to follow, but here goes: relax. Go with the fall. If you've warmed up, you should be loose enough to let your body go. Some nasty falls can happen when a skater falls backward and stiffens and the back of his or her head hits the ice. If you relax, your bottom will hit the ice first. It's much more cushioned than your head, and a safer place to land.

To get up from a fall, roll over so that you are facing the ice: you should be on your hands and knees. Now, keeping your palms on the ice, draw one foot up under you, then the other. Push yourself up with your hands, keeping your weight over your skates. Straighten your knees slowly as you go. You'll find yourself back on your feet and ready to go forward again.

Don't try to rise with your back and your bottom still facing the ice. Your feet will merely slide forward and you will sit down again, hard.

LEARNING TO PUSH AND GLIDE

By now you've been around the rink a few times. Perhaps you've even made it once or twice without holding on. You've probably practiced falling and getting up again. You're ready to learn the basic forward motion of figure skating: how to stroke, or push and glide.

Start by standing still and facing the direction in which you plan to skate. Stand tall. Get the feel of being balanced. Bend your knees slightly and keep your weight over your skates. Your arms should be at your sides, elbows tucked in, and the palms of your hands facing the ice. It might help to imagine you are resting your hands on a table that's about waist-high.

You can begin by standing with feet parallel, toes pointing forward, or you can try to begin from the T position. Your right foot will be the stem of the T. It should be facing forward. Your left foot will be the cross bar. Bring it behind the right foot so that your left instep touches your right heel (1). Just be sure you don't step on the back of your right blade.

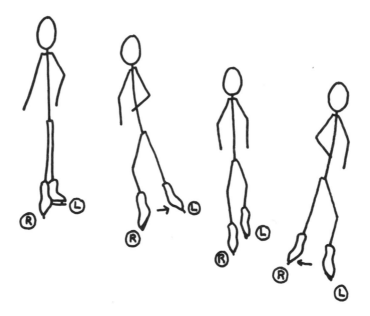

Now put your weight on your right foot and bend your right knee. Push firmly with the side of your left blade against the ice (2). You should glide forward, flat on the blade of your right skate. Gradually, straighten your right knee as you move forward. Keep your left leg behind you slightly, with the left foot pointed toward the ice. As your glide slows down, bend your right knee again slightly.

Bring your left foot up beside the right on the ice.(3). Shift your weight to your left leg, and push yourself forward by pushing with the side of your right blade firmly against the ice (4). You will be pushing out to the side this time, not directly behind you. Keep your head up and your back straight. Bend your left knee, rise, and bring your right leg forward. When your two feet are side by side, shift your weight to your right leg. Push with the side of your left blade against the ice.

Keep practicing the push and glide until the movement feels natural and easy. Keep your knees flexible and your arms well-positioned. You'll soon look like a pro.

HOW TO STOP

There are easier, more graceful, ways to stop than falling or crashing into the boards.

The Snowplow. Begin with the Snowplow, the most basic stop. Often used by beginners, the Snowplow is easy to learn and quite effective.

Glide forward on both feet, keeping your feet parallel, about a foot and a half apart. Bend your knees. Shift your weight back slightly, and push your heels apart as you turn your toes inward. You're going for the pigeon-toed look.

Drop your ankles slightly toward the ice. As you do, the inside edges of your blades will bite into the ice and help you skid to a stop. Be sure you practice this move slowly. If you bring your toes in too fast, you will end up head-first over your feet. Take your time!

The T Stop. The T stop is more professional-looking than the snowplow. It's a little harder to learn but well worth the effort.

As you skate forward on one foot—let's say your right—bring the other foot, your left, up behind, into the T position. Lower the back blade to the ice, being careful not to put your foot down on your right blade.

Now lean back on your left blade slightly. You are pressing the inside edge of the back blade into the ice. You should skid to a stop.

DEALING WITH CROWDS

Once you're up and skating, you will realize how hard it is to work your way around a crowded rink without crashing into other skaters. While you are learning, other skaters make room for you. But the better you get on skates, the more responsibility you have to look out for beginners and to prevent accidents.

What can you do?

- Always travel in the direction of traffic—usually counterclockwise.
- Stay away from other skaters. Don't push.
- Stay alert. Always look in the direction you're skating.
- If you're skating backward, check behind you frequently. Remember that skaters may stop or fall suddenly, becoming dangerous obstacles in your path.
- Learn to stop quickly.
- Expect people to cut in front of you. Be prepared to stop.
- Don't make matters worse by skating much faster than the crowd, or much slower. Try to skate the average speed.
- Don't roughhouse or engage in horseplay.
- If you feel yourself about to fall, don't grab at another skater to steady yourself. Chances are you'll both go down. Just fall.
- If you do fall, get up quickly.
- If you're really steady on your feet, by all means stop to help another skater up. But if you're unsteady, your "help" will make matters worse.
- Stay away from skaters practicing tricky moves. The center of the rink is usually reserved for figures, spins, and jumps.

Once you are moving forward with confidence, it's time to learn some fancier footwork.

5
GETTING FANCY

Since most fancy footwork involves skating on one edge of your blade at a time, it is important to learn more about edges. Each blade is sharpened so that it has two edges: an inside and an outside. Inside and outside refer to whether the side of the blade faces inside, toward the other foot, or outside, away from the body.

Standing still, you have four edges: left inside, right inside, left outside, right outside. You can either move forward or backward on any of your four edges. When skating teachers or instruction manuals describe a move, they rarely say, "Skate forward on your right outside edge." Instead, the direction you are moving becomes part of the name of the edge: "Skate on your right forward outside edge." So you actually have a total of eight edges you can skate, four on each foot.

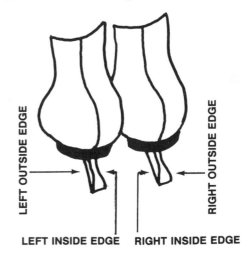

LEFT OUTSIDE EDGE

RIGHT OUTSIDE EDGE

LEFT INSIDE EDGE   RIGHT INSIDE EDGE

38

LFO	Left forward outside	RFO	Right forward outside
LBO	Left backward outside	RBO	Right backward outside
LFI	Left forward inside	RFI	Right forward inside
LBI	Left backward inside	RBI	Right backward inside

GETTING A FEEL
FOR YOUR EDGES

Now that you know what they're called, try to get a feel for your edges by skating forward swizzles.

To start, take a few gliding steps and then bring your feet parallel and together. Now slowly let your toes separate as you keep your knees together. Then let your blades fall onto an inside edge by dropping your ankles slightly toward the ice. You'll know you've found that inside edge when your toes begin to head toward one another. Bring your feet parallel, and try again until you can find your inside edges automatically.

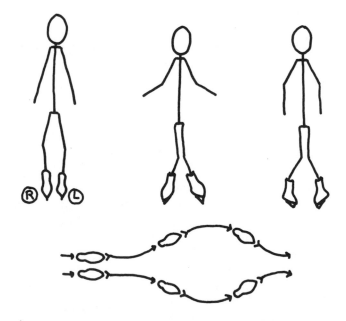

Now try skating forward on both feet. Bend your left knee slightly and lean your body, all of a piece, into an imaginary circle. Don't bend from your feet, your waist, or your ankles. If you're doing it correctly, you will curve to the left. You will be skating on your left forward outside edge. Now bend your right knee slightly and lean into the center of an imaginary circle to your right. You should curve to the right. You are skating on your right forward outside edge.

Leaning "all of piece" is important to good figure skating form. If you ride a bicycle, you know you have to lean your whole body when you steer the bike around curves. It's very much the same in skating. Lean your whole body to the left when you want to curve to the left. Lean your whole body to the right when you want to curve to the right.

If you still have trouble with the idea of leaning all of a piece, imagine a line running down the center of your body as you stand erect. Now tilt that whole line, as if you were the Tower of Pisa. You should be skating on one of your outside edges if you are leaning correctly.

FORWARD CROSSOVERS

To get more practice with edges, and to learn how to handle curves—such as those at the corners of the rink—it's helpful to learn crossovers. These sound much harder than they are. You might find it easier to practice the foot movements a few times without skates, on the floor, before you try this on the ice.

Skate forward on your left foot. Lean "all of a piece" to your left, so that you are skating on your left outside edge (LFO). You should be curving toward the left.

Bring your right foot up close to your left foot. Now pass your right foot in front of and over the left. Put your right blade down on the ice close to your left foot. At this point, your ankles will be

crossed. Both knees should be bent when the actual "crossover" is happening.

Now shift your weight onto your right leg, and use your left foot to push yourself forward. Lift up your left foot and bring it behind your skating foot—your right foot. You should now be skating forward on your right inside edge (RFI). You will still be curving to the left.

Bring your left foot up beside your right. To keep going, you will automatically push with the right skate as you shift your weight to your left leg. You are now skating forward on your left foot on the outside edge, and you are ready to do another crossover, or to continue pushing and gliding.

Since traffic at most rinks travels counterclockwise, the crossover described above will be most useful to you as you turn corners. But to learn all your edges, try doing crossovers in the other direction, too. (RFO—cross—to LFI). You can also do crossovers while skating backward.

SKATING BACKWARD:
A TWO-FOOTED APPROACH

Besides being fun and looking impressive, skating backward is wonderfully useful. Many advanced skating moves start from a backward position, and a great many more end there.

The simplest way to skate backward is called backward swizzles, or sculling. While it's not terribly graceful or speedy, it will give you the feeling of moving backward on skates. And it's very easy to learn.

Start by standing pigeon-toed, so that your toes point to one another. Your heels should be slanting out. Bend your knees in slightly, and push your feet apart as you rise. You'll move backward slowly. Your heels will slide out and back, and your toes will move away from one another.

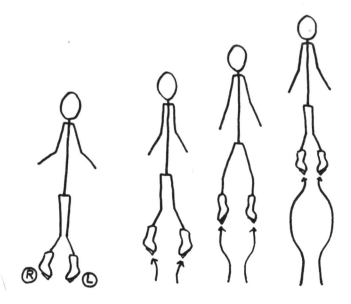

When your toes are about 18 inches apart, try to bring your heels together by pulling in with the insides of the thighs. As your feet get closer, bend your knees, and try to aim your toes at each other again. Take your time and prepare before doing the next one, rather than trying to do too many too quickly. If you are sculling correctly, you'll be creating a tracing on the ice that looks something like the drawing below.

While you're sculling, or swizzling, and getting the feel of moving backward, be sure to practice looking over your shoulder. You don't want to bump into someone—or something, like the wall!

SKATING BACKWARD:
ONE FOOT AT A TIME

Now you're ready to try skating backward the way the pros do it—on one foot at a time.

Stand with your feet about 12 inches apart. Your arms should be at your sides, elbows tucked in, palms facing the ice. Turn your arms slightly toward the right (1).

Shift your weight to your left foot and lift your right foot. Bring your right foot in beside the left, and move your arms slightly to the left (2). Now use your left blade to make a rounded cut in the ice in front of you. This cut is your push backward. As you make it, shift your weight to your right leg and turn your shoulders to the right (3).

You should be moving backward. As you glide, bring your left foot in toward your right foot along the ice. When the left heel points toward the right toe, lift your left foot off the ice. Straighten your left knee as your skate leaves the ice. To add a graceful look, point your left toe toward the ice (4).

Now you are slowing down as you glide backward on your right foot. You need to push again, to keep your momentum and speed going. Bring your left foot alongside and parallel to the

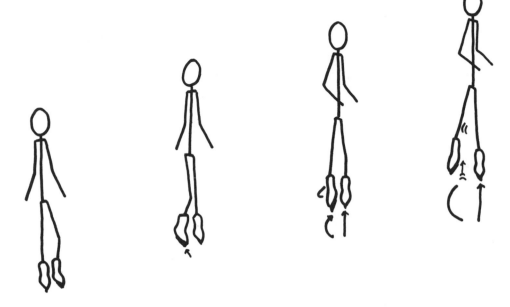

right (5). Bend your right knee, and turn the heel of your right skate outward (6). Pushing hard with your blade against the ice, make a curved cut along the ice with your right blade as you shift your weight to your left foot and bend your left knee (7). Bring your right heel in toward your left toe, and lift your right foot off the ice (8). You should be gliding backward on your left foot now, with your right foot in front of you, pointing toward the ice.

This sounds much more complicated than it really is, but the moves will take some practice. Be sure to push off strongly when you make the curved cut along the ice. Keep your back straight and your knees flexible. And don't forget to check over your shoulders from time to time! If you can get a friend to watch the traffic for you while you try to skate backward, it will go more easily for you.

A SIMPLE TURN:
THE THREE TURN

The three turn is named for the figure you trace in the ice when you do it correctly. It also takes three positions to do it, so its name can help you remember the three-step procedure. It's a simple turn, easy to learn and fun to do. Be sure you can skate backward on one foot quite well before you try it, though.

First, try a forward three-turn. You will start skating forward on your left outside edge (LFO).

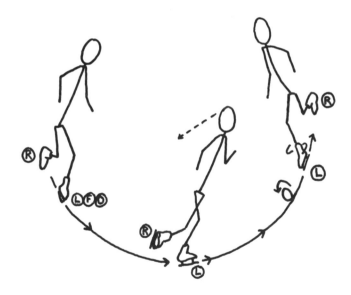

Bring your right arm, shoulder, and hip forward and press your left arm, shoulder, and hip back. Your right foot should be back, off the ice, with the toe pointed down.

You should now be skating in a curve. Imagine the circle this curve is part of. Look at the center of this circle, and flip your left skate around as your foot turns. Press your right arm, shoulder, and hip back and continue to look into the circle. You should finish this three turn on a left back inside (LBI) edge.

THE SPIRAL

The spiral is simple to do but it looks very impressive. It's the ice-skating version of ballet's arabesque. A well-done spiral will always get attention. At the same time, it can help you practice your edges and perfect your balance and control.

Some skaters find it helpful to practice the spiral while standing at the boards. Facing the boards, they put both hands out to the side, hold on, and bend forward at the waist. They look as if they wanted to rest their chins on the barrier. At the same time, they also lift one foot off the ice, stretching the back lifted leg as far as it will go. They turn the lifted foot out and keep their heads up.

Of course, this is more difficult to do when you are moving. If you'd like to try, skate forward on one foot—say your left forward outside edge (LFO). Lift your right leg behind you as you lean forward from the waist. Stretch your arms out beside your shoulders for balance, keeping your palms facing the ice.

You can practice this move with an adult skating beside you on two feet and holding one of your hands. The support might give you enough confidence to lift your leg and give the spiral a try. If you have a willing—and steady—grown-up nearby, ask for a hand.

If you don't have someone to help you, try practicing the spiral with your leg lifted only slightly above the ice. When you feel strong and balanced at that height, try the spiral again and again with your leg lifted higher each time.

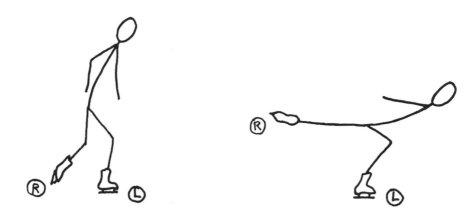

Once you learn how to balance on one leg for the spiral, work on your form. For a good-looking spiral, lift your head, arch your back, and keep your lifted leg as straight as you can. Turn the toe out and press your heel down.

A SIMPLE JUMP:
THE WALTZ JUMP

If you are steady on your skates and can skate forward and backward on your edges, consider learning a waltz jump. A waltz jump is a half turn you make in the air as you skate forward on one foot, jump and turn, and land, skating backward on the other foot.

Start by skating forward on your left outside edge (LFO). Drop your arms a little, and bend your left leg. Keep your right shoulder forward. Now throw your right leg forward and up. This will pull all of your right side up, too. If you lift your arms when you throw your free leg, you will jump even higher. But it would not be

48

a good idea to jump too high the first few times you try a waltz jump.

While you are in the air, you will be switching your hip position so that you can land skating backward on the outside edge of your right skate (RBO). Your knee must be bent when you land.

You will land on the bottom tooth of the toe pick, but as soon as you've landed, shift your weight back a little further to the middle of the blade. Not landing on the toe pick might mean slipping off the edge. Staying on the toe pick too long after landing will cause you to fall.

Your left arm should be in front of you, your right arm extended to the side as you land. Keep your body straight, but remember to keep your landing knee bent. Keep your shoulders steady to stop your body from turning at the end of the jump.

A SIMPLE
TWO-FOOTED SPIN

For a final bit of showmanship, you can try a simple spin. This one lets you stay on two feet, so you can get used to spinning without worrying too much about balance.

Stand with your feet about a foot apart. Put your weight over your left toe, and turn your head and shoulders to the right. Now throw your arms and shoulders to the left as you bring your right foot around and close to the left. Drop onto the flat of your blades, bring your arms close to your body, and see if you're spinning.

ADVANCED JUMPS,
SPINS, AND POSITIONS

The moves described in this chapter are used primarily in free-style skating. You will notice as you watch advanced skaters that there are many other types of jumps and spins. Here are a few you might see either at your rink or on televised skating events such as the National or World Championships or the Winter Olympics.

Arabian—a flying spin done from a two-footed takeoff.

Axel—a jump invented by Axel Paulsen. The skater turns one and one half times in the air, as he or she jumps from a forward outside edge and lands on the back outside edge of the other foot. In addition to the basic axel, there are double axels (two and a half revolutions in the air) and triple axels (three and a half revolutions in the air).

Camel—a spin done on one foot in the spiral, or arabesque, position.

Flip—a one-revolution jump. The skater uses the toe pick to assist the takeoff.

Flying camel—a flying spin landing in a back camel.

Loop jump—another one-revolution jump. The skater takes off from a back outside edge and lands on the back outside edge of the same foot.

Lutz—a toe-assisted jump. Takeoff is from a back outside edge. Landing is on the back outside edge of the toe-assisting foot.

Russian split—the skater touches his or her toes during a split jump.

Salchow—a one-revolution jump with takeoff from a back inside edge. Landing is on the back outside edge of the opposite foot. Invented by Ulrich Salchow, this jump is now done in double and triple versions as well.

Spread eagle—a two-footed glide. The feet are in alignment with each other, with heels facing and toes pointed out.

Walley—a one-revolution jump. Takeoff is from a back inside edge. Landing is on the back outside edge of the same foot.

These jumps, spins, and positions are more difficult and more dangerous than those described fully in this chapter. It would be wise to get advice from a professional figure skating instructor before trying these more advanced moves.

6
CUCCING A FIGURE

Freestyle skating is beautiful, but there's more to figure skating than jumps and spins. Any skater who is serious about competing must also learn to trace figures on the ice with skill and precision.

Skaters need to learn many figures. The simplest is called the circle eight, or figure eight. As its name implies, the figure eight is actually two circles whose edges touch to form the number 8. You can skate the circle eight on your inside or your outside edges, but you always begin on your right foot. Each time you skate a figure, try to skate right over your original tracing on the ice.

Find a large, clear area of the ice in which to work. Each circle of your eight should be three times as tall as you are. If you are four feet tall, for example, each circle should measure twelve feet from top to bottom and from side to side. You will need twelve feet of clear ice in front of you and twelve feet behind. You will most likely find the space you need in the middle of the rink. It's best if the ice is relatively unmarked so you can see your tracings clearly.

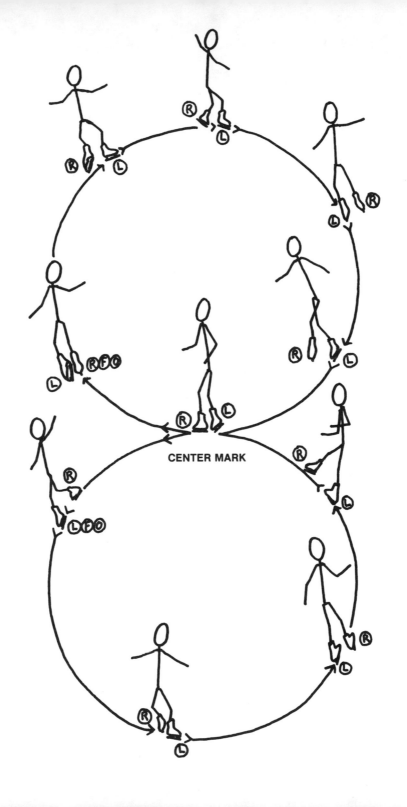

CENTER MARK

Stand at the middle of the space you have chosen and mark a small cross in the ice with the toe pick of one of your skates. This is your starting mark, where you begin and return to. When you become more advanced and comfortable skating eights you won't need this mark, but for now it can be helpful. Before you skate a stroke, imagine the figure you are about to cut. Try to see the circle you will trace in your mind's eye.

Let's say you will skate this eight RFO–LFO. Stand at your center mark, with your right forward outside edge on the line at which your circles will touch. Picture the circle again. Now, with your weight over your left foot, bend your right knee and push yourself forward onto your right outside edge.

Lean into the circle, keeping your right hand over the line you are about to trace, your left arm behind you. Your left foot should also be behind you, with your heel over the line you have traced already. Hold this pose for about the first third of the distance around your circle.

Keeping your left hip, shoulder, and arm back, *slowly* bring your left leg and foot forward. This swing should take the next third of the circle to complete. When you are two-thirds of the way around, allow your left shoulder, hip, and arm to come forward, too, until you are squarely facing the direction in which you are traveling. As your body comes around, you should slowly rise on your right knee.

When you come back around to the center, your starting point, bring both feet together, bend your knees, and turn your hips and shoulders so that you are ready and able to strike out on your left forward outside edge.

Again, hold your position for the first third of the way around the circle. Bring your free leg—the right leg—slowly forward for the second third. During the final third of the circle, allow your body to face the tracing. You will come back to the center of your figure eight, and are ready to begin again.

7
EVOLVING A STYLE

Once you've mastered the basics of figure skating, it's time to think about style. Style isn't so much what you do, it's how you do it. It's the extra something you add, the signature that makes each move yours.

So how do you go about evolving a style? In skating, as in other activities, style should be an expression of who you are. And in skating, as in any sport, who you are means not only what your personality is like, but also what your body type is.

START WITH BODY TYPE

No one body type makes a perfect skater. Different body types make different kinds of wonderful skaters. Think for a moment about Olympic gold medalist Dorothy Hamill. She's five feet, three inches tall, and at the 1976 Winter Olympics weighed 120 pounds. The 1968 Olympic winner, Peggy Fleming, is taller and more slender than Hamill. Hamill's compact build lends itself to a more athletic, dramatic kind of performance, while Fleming's wil-

56

*Dorothy Hamill, the 1976 Olympic
figure skating champion*

lowy body is perfect for the kinds of graceful, lyrical, fluid moves she is justly famous for.

Two other skaters to look for are Katarina Witt of East Germany, who won gold medals at the 1987 World Championships and the 1984 Winter Olympics, and an up-and-coming East German pair skater, Ekaterina Gordeeva. Witt stands five feet, five inches tall and weighs 114 pounds. Gordeeva weighs just 77 pounds and stands a petite four feet, ten inches. Different builds, different kinds of skaters.

What about *your* body type? Are you built low to the ground, with powerful legs—the sort of build that makes for high jumps and powerhouse spins? Or are you tall and thin—the graceful, languid type? Tall skaters often make wonderful ice dancers. Maybe you're very athletic, like some of the powerful German skaters. Or diminutive and impish—think of Scott Hamilton. Whatever your body type, you can find a style that suits you.

PERSONALITY

Your temperament should also be reflected in your skating style. It may contrast or match your body type. Watch skating performances and compare the mood of each. While each freestyle program should include a range of moods, there should be a dominant feeling. Some skaters seem jazzy and energized, others dreamy and romantic. Some seem down to earth, others almost angelic. What parts of yourself would you like to express through skating?

The kinds of music you like could be one key to your personal style. Try skating in time to the music played at the rink. There

Katarina Witt, the 1987
world figure skating champion

should be a range—everything from old waltzes and classical pieces to show tunes, rock, and disco. Try to choreograph your own moves to the music.

Watching skating competitions on television or in person, or attending a show such as the Ice Capades, can give you some ideas on music and personality. You will see skaters performing as flamenco dancers, Hungarian peasants, even belly dancers. Music will range from Michael Jackson to Gershwin to Mozart.

If you're skating outdoors, or want to try your own kind of music, you can wear a personal tape player or radio and earphones as you work out. Just be sure your music machine is firmly fastened to your body. You don't want your cassette player or radio hitting the ice. It could break—or, worse, hurt someone who might skate over it.

If you're really serious about developing a style, here are two additional hints. First, try to skate where there's a full mirrored wall—similar to those you see in ballet studios. Skating where you can watch yourself will help you develop gestures that will enhance your style.

Second, use a video. Get a friend or a parent to tape your skating. Study your performance. What could you do better? Do you need to bend your knees more deeply, keep your arms up higher, lengthen your neck and keep your head up straight? One videotaped session will give you enough information for hours of additional practice.

You can also videotape skaters whose performances are broadcast on television, if you have a VCR. Watch these tapes again and again, looking for clues to style. You can even watch them in slow motion if your VCR has that capacity, so you'll really understand how every move is made.

If you are thinking hard about style, and have mastered all the basic figure skating moves, perhaps you are ready to test your abilities through competition.

8
COMPETITIONS AND CAREERS

Some young skaters will perfect their moves, develop their styles, and skate for the sheer fun of it for the rest of their lives. Others will become paid professional ice skaters, working in ice shows as clowns, chorus members—maybe even stars. Still others will go on to amateur competitions, perhaps winning a place on the national figure skating team and competing in World Championships, or even the Winter Olympics.

When should you begin skating if you plan to have a competitive or a professional career? Most experts say you should start between the ages of 6 and 10. But don't call it quits if you're 11 and just starting. Young people up to the age of 15 who are quick learners, well coordinated, and ambitious still have plenty of time to learn how to skate.

No matter what age you begin skating, you will have to be serious if you want to compete and succeed. It will take discipline, dedication, time, and money. Outfits, skates, lessons, ice time, coaching, and travel to contests all require cash. Parents and families of successful skaters often sacrifice other interests—everything from vacations to college educations—to pay for the skater's career.

The skater makes other sacrifices. Between school, sleep, and skating, there's rarely time for other interests. Dates, dances, and movies take a back seat to workouts, lessons, and practice. Skaters also watch their diets closely: ice cream, hamburgers, and french fries become forbidden foods.

Skaters with ambitions usually work with a coach who helps them to define their goals and set up a training schedule. That schedule can be grueling, with 16 to 24 hours of skating each week.

And on-ice practice is only part of it. Most skaters also spend at least an hour a day doing a workout off the ice. These off-ice sessions help the skater build strength, develop concentration and control, and enhance versatility. Weight training and dance classes—in classical ballet, jazz, and modern dance—might all be part of a champion's regimen.

TESTS AND COMPETITIONS

In the United States, two organizations conduct tests and competitions for skaters. If you are serious about skating, you will probably want to join one of these groups. Both have very reasonable membership fees. Which one you join will depend on your goals as a skater.

If you are interested in recreational skating, or a paid career as a skater, you would probably join the Ice Skating Institute of America, known as the ISIA. If you are interested in competing as an amateur, and perhaps becoming part of the national team and going to the Olympics, the U.S. Figure Skating Association, or USFSA, is the group for you. The USFSA conducts competitions and tests for amateurs—from the most inexperienced skaters to Olympic hopefuls.

OLYMPIC CHAMPIONS:
PAST, PRESENT, AND FUTURE

Winning the National Championship is wonderful, winning the World Championship is super, but the Olympics have a unique status. To be an Olympic medalist is the dream of many figure skaters.

The United States has in the past produced many Olympic medalists. Dick Button won the Olympic gold medal in 1948 and again in 1952. In the 1956 Winter Olympics, another American, Tenley Albright, won the women's gold medal. Albright went on to become a surgeon. The 1956 Olympic silver medalist, U.S. skater Carol Heiss, became the gold medal winner at the 1960 Olympic Games in Squaw Valley.

Peggy Fleming captured the hearts of the Olympic crowd and the gold medal for the USA in 1968, while another super U.S. skater, Janet Lynn, took the bronze. Dorothy Hamill won the gold for the USA in 1976, and Linda Fratianne took the silver in 1980.

Among recent men's Olympic competitors, John Curry, who won the gold for Great Britain in 1976, and Toller Cranston, who won the bronze medal for Canada the same year, stand out. Curry is known for taking his inspiration from classical ballet, while Cranston is famous for his innovative and dramatic moves.

In the 1984 Winter Olympics at Sarajevo, Scott Hamilton, World Champion in 1981, 1982, 1983, and 1984, won the gold medal for the U.S. Hamilton has turned pro since then and will not be a contender in the 1988 Olympics. But Katarina Witt might skate to keep her crown during the 1988 Olympic games in Calgary, Alberta, Canada.

Other female skaters who might compete in the 1988 Olympic games include Tiffany Chin, the 1985 United States champion. Chin skated with great power and purity of line in 1985, but a muscle problem forced her off the ice for a year. Whether she will compete in the 1988 Olympics remains a question.

Right:
Scott Hamilton
Below:
Peggy Fleming
Facing page:
Debi Thomas,
the silver medalist
in the 1987 World
Championships

Midori Ito,
another top skater

Debi Thomas, the first black National Champion, number one in the 1986 World Championships, and number two in the 1987 World Championships, also stands a chance in Calgary, especially if she includes five flawless triple jumps in her program—a feat she has managed in the past. Two women to watch are Caryn Kadavy, an American skater of stunning elegance, and Elizabeth Manley, the 1985 Canadian champion. Kira Ivanova, Claudia Leistner, and Midori Ito are three other women to watch.

In the Olympic men's figure skating event, look for Canada's Brian Orser, who placed second in the 1984 Olympics and first in the 1987 World Championships. Moscow's Alexandr Fadeev might also be a contender. At the World Championships, his triple Lutz and triple toe-loop combination, triple axel, and double toe-loop wowed the crowds. Christopher Bowman is another skater many feel has a chance of winning a medal.

U.S. skater Brian Boitano, a bronze medalist in the 1984 Olympics, World Champion in 1985 and 1986, and runner-up in the 1987 World Championships, is another one to watch. Boitano is something of a history maker: in 1982, at the age of 18, he was the U.S. male to do a triple axel in the U.S. nationals. In the 1983 world's competition, his program included an incredible six triple jumps.

YOUR FUTURE ON SKATES

You might dream of skating your way to an Olympic medal, to fame and fortune, or to a job in an ice review. Or maybe your goals are more modest: to skate safely around the rink, to skate backward, to perfect a few simple jumps and spins.

Whatever your goals, by now you've taken the first glides toward reaching them. You've also begun learning a sport you can practice and enjoy throughout your life. Skating can help keep you both fit and happy. Just remember to skate safely, and don't forget to have fun!

FOR FURTHER READING

Dolan, Edward F. *Dorothy Hamill, Olympic Skating Champion.* New York: Doubleday, 1979.

Fassi, Carlo. *Figure Skating with Carlo Fassi*. New York: Scribner, 1980.

Harris, Ricky. *Choreography and Style for Ice Skaters*. New York: St. Martin's Press, 1980.

Krementz, Jill. *A Very Young Skater*. New York: Knopf, 1979.

Money, Keith. *John Curry*. New York: Knopf, 1978.

Petkevich, John Misha. *The Skater's Handbook*. New York: Scribner, 1984.

Steere, Michael. *Scott Hamilton*. New York: St. Martin's Press, 1985.

Strait, Raymond. *Queen of Ice, Queen of Shadows: The Unsuspected Life of Sonja Henie*. New York: Stein and Day, 1985.

Torvill, Jayne. *Torvill and Dean*. New York: St. Martin's Press, 1983.

Van Steenwyk, Elizabeth. *Figure Skating*. New York: Harvey House, 1976.

Van Steenwyk, Elizabeth. *Peggy Fleming*. New York: McGraw Hill, 1978.

Wright, Benjamin T. *Reader's Guide to Figure Skating's Hall of Fame*. Boston: United States Figure Skating Association, 1978.

INDEX